# Stay Safe!
# Out and about

Lisa Bruce

Heinemann
LIBRARY

Little Nippers

**www.heinemann.co.uk/library**
Visit our website to find out more information about **Heinemann Library** books.

To order:
☎ Phone 44 (0) 1865 888066
▤ Send a fax to 44 (0) 1865 314091
▢ Visit the Heinemann Bookshop at www.heinemann.co.uk/library to browse our catalogue and order online.

First published in Great Britain by Heinemann Library, Halley Court, Jordan Hill, Oxford OX2 8EJ, part of Harcourt Education.
Heinemann is a registered trademark of Harcourt Education Ltd.

Editorial: Jilly Attwood and Claire Throp
Design: Jo Hinton-Malivoire and bigtop, Bicester, UK
Models made by: Jo Brooker
Picture Research: Rosie Garai
Production: Séverine Ribierre

Originated by Dot Gradations
Printed and bound in China by South China Printing Company

ISBN 0 431 17273 0 (hardback)
07 06 05 04 03
10 9 8 7 6 5 4 3 2 1

ISBN 0 431 17278 1 (paperback)
07 06 05 04 03
10 9 8 7 6 5 4 3 2 1

**British Library Cataloguing in Publication Data**
Bruce, Lisa
Stay safe out and about – (Little Nippers)
363.1
A full catalogue record for this book is available from the British Library.

**Acknowledgements**
The publishers would like to thank the following for permission to reproduce photographs: Collections pp. **8** (Sophia Skyers), **9** (Ashley Cooper), **12–13** (John D Beldom), **23** (Roger Scruton); Gareth Boden p. **7**; Greg Evans Photo Library pp. **18–19**, **20–21**; Photofusion p. **14–15** (Leslie Garland); Trevor Clifford pp. **4–5**, **10**; Trip p. **17** (J. Ellard).

Cover photograph reproduced with permission of Masterfile/Rommel.

The publishers would like to thank Annie Davy for her assistance in the preparation of this book.

Every effort has been made to contact copyright holders of any material reproduced in this book. Any omissions will be rectified in subsequent printings if notice is given to the publishers.

# Contents

# Safety when you're out

To stay safe there are a few things you need to watch out for.

# Buckle up

What do Jamie and Lisa have in the car to keep them safe?

Click

Car seat

Seat belt

# Empty buildinys

Empty buildings are
very dangerous
to play in.

# Where is a safe place to play?

Remember to always play where grown-ups can see you.

Say NO
to strangers

Someone Kelly doesn't know asks her to go with him. She should say **NO** and tell a grown-up.

# Water

Lakes, rivers and ponds are exciting places to visit.

What might happen if you play too near the edge?

13

# Cross safely

Bridge

How would you get to the other side of the stream?

# Ice is slippery

Snow and ice can be very **slippery**.

Whooosh!

# Railways

It is very
dangerous to play
near trains and
railway lines.

# Play safely

What are these children doing that is dangerous?

# Follow the rules

Follow these rules
Make a start
You'll stay safe
And you'll be smart!

# Index

The end

## Notes for adults

*Stay Safe!* supports young children's knowledge and understanding of the world around them. The four books will help children to connect safely with the ever-expanding world in which they find themselves. The following Early Learning Goals are relevant to this series:
• move with confidence, imagination and in safety
• move with control and co-ordination
• show awareness of space, of themselves and of others
• use a range of small and large equipment
• handle tools, objects, construction and malleable materials safely and with increasing control
• understand what is right, what is wrong, and why
• dress and undress independently and manage their own personal hygiene.

The *Stay Safe!* series will help children to think more about the potential dangers they will face as they grow up. Discussion can be focused on what makes an activity safe or unsafe allowing the children to learn how to protect themselves from harm. The books can be used to help children understand how their own behaviour can make a difference to their safety.

**Out and about** will help children extend their vocabulary, as they will hear new words such as *buckle, empty, buildings, dangerous, strangers, exciting, safely* and *slippery.*

### Follow-up activities
• Teach the children that the safest way to cross a road is to use the Green Cross Code i.e. find a safe place to cross, look both ways and listen for cars, and when there is no traffic, walk straight across while continuing to look both ways.
• Create a park on a large sheet of paper and draw in a pond, playground, old building, trees and river with bridge etc. Ask the children which areas are safe and which are dangerous in their imaginary park.